More Fit for Gills Than Lungs:
A Collection of Poetry

Sara Preston

More Fit for Gills Than Lungs: A Collection
of Poetry © 2022

Sara Preston

All rights reserved.

No part of this publication may be
reproduced, stored in a retrieval system, or
transmitted, in any form or by any means,
electronic, mechanical, photocopying,
recording or otherwise, without the prior
written permission of the presenters.

Sara Preston asserts the moral right to be
identified as the author of this work.

Presentation by *BookLeaf Publishing*

Web: www.bookleafpub.com

E-mail: info@bookleafpub.com

ISBN: 9798438805366

First edition 2022

To my darling Mum, Dad, and sisters.

My family, my heart, my refuge.

Thank you always for your unconditional love.

ACKNOWLEDGEMENT

To Craig, Euan, and all my friends who have heard snippets over the years (when I felt enough temporary confidence to share).
I wouldn't have gotten here, be alive, or be me - without you.
To the castle, for leaving a light on - thank you with all my heart.

PREFACE

This is a place to collect the spattering of words,
poetry and thoughts that have gathered together
in a little bundle over time and continue to make
new – on a path through mental illness – and the
ongoing trek to positive health, wellbeing and
recovery.

Sometimes a reflection of painful times gone by,
sometimes a note to my younger self, sometimes
an expression of an internal struggle or joyful
moment, sometimes a stern conversation with an
affliction I have bid farewell.

And finally, sometimes just a broken spattering
of words, that with each uttering and scribe has
helped give me hope and healing – and perhaps
can do so for someone, somewhere else, too.

"To love life, to love it even
when you have no stomach for it
and everything you've held dear
crumbles like burnt paper in your hands,
your throat filled with the silt of it.
When grief sits with you, its tropical heat
thickening the air, heavy as water
more fit for gills than lungs;
when grief weighs you like your own flesh

only more of it, an obesity of grief,
you think, how can a body withstand this?
Then you hold life like a face
between your palms, a plain face,
no charming smile, no violet eyes,
and you say, yes, I will take you
I will love you, again." - Ellen Bass.

Band Aid

It is the scab that will not heal,
it is the itch that will not ease,
it is the hole that will not fill,
it is the thing that keeps me ill.

Blanket

Can I ask you to place a blanket,
over me and all the hurt?
To cocoon me with your safety,
to preserve our efforts, not exert?
Could I ask you to sit with me,
in the transition still?
From little grub,
to finding wings,
I may take flight,
aft' all years ill.

The Scarlet Letter "A"

Run, run, run. Running to, running from?
Away? Pounding and grasping.
Clinging on for dear life. Is this living?
Routine. The daily grind. Grind my bones. Grit
my teeth.

Run until exhaustion. Daybreak to night. No
light.
Consumption is light – as a feather. Nothing
more.
I'm consumed. Tentatively balancing on the
brink. Of death or life?
Intake, burn, output – don't pass out.

Hold balance and poise.Hate balancing –
balances, scales, weight.
Wait. Life's at full speed, my tank's half empty.
Never full. I'm never full. Hungry.
On standby, logged out, shut down, hibernation.
Sedate.

Streamlined, slim, and slick.
Efficient, perfect.
Sick?
Gracile, agile, docile, hostile.
A host for something else?

A parasite, not me.
Obsessive, regimented, to the letter.
The scarlet letter. "A".
"A" for guilt, shame and hopelessness.

Branded with a mark. The stain of illness.
Written all over my face.
Wearing the disorder head to toe.
No freedom, no escape.
Embodying the form.
A form of torture, punishment, entrapment.
No concealment, no hiding place, no break.
Until I break. It breaks.

When?
Let it be soon, let it be now, let it be over.
Will it ever end?
What is life, what was life, who was I, who am I
now?
I can't stop it, I can't beat it.
So I wait until my heart stops beating.
Wait? Wait. Just wait.
Just weight.

Dear Body

Dear Body,
I'm sorry.
For all that it put you and I through.
The pain and affliction,
the magnitude of the depths,
the indescribable torment.

Dear Body,
I'm sorry.
For letting it take you to the very threshold of
your capabilities,
the brink of your fortitude.
For trying to destroy us.
I don't know how you coped,
or survived to function?
When it made us so weak?
I couldn't.

Dear Body,
I'm sorry.
It must have been so hard for you,
to be left an empty vessel,
as I became a silenced soul.
When you were only a tired frame of palpable
bones.

Our fingers singed with frozen blood, cold to
touch, no fuel to stoke the fire.
And sunken sockets in shades of silver; lips of
lilac, only passing breath.
The light in our eyes- all but extinguished.
You changed, and I changed too.

Dear Body,
I'm sorry.
That I couldn't fight it sooner.

Dear Body,
Thank you.
For waiting for me.
For holding on when there wasn't much of you
left.
For persevering,
for getting me,
[for getting us] through.

Dear Body,
Thank you.
For coming back fighting,
even after failing.
Even when the disease made you shut down.
For loving me,
even when our mind battled against you.
Tortured you.

Dear Body,
Thank you.
For doing everything in your power to help us
survive.

Dear Body,
I love you.
Although we still bear scars,
not physical or visible to the eye.
Although our bones are aged and porous,
our heart still healing,
our mind adjusting.
We made it,
you and I.

Dear Body,
I love you.
And I will fight for you,
just as you fought for me.
Because, you are the keeper of my soul,
the refuge our heart and mind calls home.
Because we deserve it,
Us.

Dear Body,
I love you.
[Always].

Empty Vessel

As a teen she could not live at home,
not well enough, and not allowed.
The shroud of death hung overhead,
threshold imminent,
tentative.

Counting down days, not marking increasing
years.
Appendages singed with frozen blood, cold to
touch.
No fuel to stoke the fire.
Reciprocal depletion, consumed and corrupted.

A body riddled with disorder.
Bereft.
Left - but a carcass,
A tired rack of flesh.

An empty vessel,
for a silenced soul.

Sharp angles, points and edges,
the arc lost its place.
Expense conquered input.
And so the house was left to waste.

When We Were Young

Take me back,
To those halcyon amber days.
When imagination held no bounds,
and time passed smoothly -
just as Mother's butter spread over morning
toast.

Take me back to when dusk came as an alarm
clock for bed.
The streetlight embers burned,
as our bedroom lights turned off.
When grass stains and grazed knees were a
badge of honour.
When frozen fingers tips and runny noses didn't
matter.

Take me back to rat-a-tat-tat,
when we knocked on doors to ask to play,
in real life,
face to face,
holding hands – no screens to keep us apart.
When we roamed each other's gardens,
Finding nature's treasures.
When we held buttercups underneath our chins,
and all we wanted - was to explore outside – not
in.

Take me back to when the only phone was on a
cord and tethered.
When we were full of adventure.
When the cold spurred us on.
When we picked the gravel out of our hands and
knees after falling,
and were okay with the scrapes and dried blood.
Proud of the scarlet additions to our uniform,
because the team and the game were more
important.
When we held handstand competitions on the
lawn,
and marvelled at the wonder of playing with
nothing –
sticks, mud, skipping ropes and chalk would
more than do.

Take me back to when the stickiness of ice- pops
clinged to our cheeks.
When we jumped the flower beds to retrieve a
ball…
all the while dodging the "town-crier's" call
from high windows,
because we'd "flattened the tulips" growing in
their garden.
When we cycled to the shops alone,
barely a decade old.
When we let go of the handlebars,

only for a passing second, that felt like a
lifetime!
Just to feel the rush and excitement –
all mashed together in a beautiful sandwich of
youth.
The high of the risk muddled with peer-driven
pride,
and the joyful ability to show off.
Sometimes falling, but never failing,
and always getting "right back on the horse."

Take me back to when the wind was in our hair,
our lungs,
our hearts,
our collective soul.
When the warm bath before bed,
held every scent and memory,
of the wondrous day we'd just lived.
Breathing each magic moment deeply,
into the safety of the evening cocoon.
When nothing was an obstacle,
and it seemed no one stood in our way.
When fear was our friend,
and the future, a distant dream.
When there was a warm embrace,
a kiss goodnight,
and the final countdown to lights off.
Take me back.
To when we were young.

Ashtray Eyes

Your ashtray eyes are no disguise,
for the wreckage and the lies inside.
They cannot hide the tears you've cried,
kohl liner carves black tracts once dried.

Pools etched pale grey, were once blue bright,
aloft dark rings of sleepless nights.
No sight of soul or glimpsing light,
just fear-fixed jet of fight or flight.

Your ashtray eyes are no disguise,
for the wreckage and the lies inside.
There's no surprise that your demise,
is chronicled in windows wise.

The smoke that floats around your head,
and chokes your throat with noose pretend,
Blocks uttered words that used to mend,
the fractured ties of long-lost friends.

Your ashtray eyes are no disguise,
for the wreckage and the lies inside.
And you despise those who remind,
of the life and times, you left behind.

Corrupted lungs as taper burns,
Exhaling all life's lessons learned,
So, each intake of breath affirms,
here marks the point of no return.

Heard

If the illness, the struggle, the fear and the pain,
Were not all trapped inside, but used for others
to gain.
So the time and the opportunities missed were
no loss,
If employed as currency, so the next bear no
cost.

If I can use my voice – have my experiences
told,
So from diagnosis, I'm not just 'a label' 'like
this' 'til I'm old,
If I can share my own negatives and turn into
good,
Without hesitation – raised hand – I'd stand up
and I would.

For this cannot continue – year after year,
A new generation living in fear,
Of the stigma, and the shortage in services
mental,
It's unjust, not enough - to be seen as
inconsequential.

But is this a pipe dream? Of a mind broken,
unstable, unsound?
No good for board meetings, handovers or
rounds?
Is my voice valid, or will I forever be 'sick?'
Am I tarnished, categorised, in a check-box now
ticked?

If I could voice what I've been through,
And have you really hear, not just listen.
With care, insight and patience,
Have you understand, not dismiss it.

And when I get to the end,
Not speak for me, what you've learned,
But be a medium and amplifier,
For my voice to be heard.

Why Does The Pain Stay With Me?

Why does the pain stay with me?
Even though the suffering is over.
The flashbacks, make me back track,
I'm caught in a limbo.
It's so clear, so raw and yet a blur,
a confusion.
Was it? Did it? Me?
It all happened, right?

I bear the marks to remind me,
scars not physical, or visible to the eye.
I've etched in ink beneath my skin,
lest we, lest I, forget.
Beauty they say, or health? Which is it?
Is only skin deep.
For violin fit I may appear,
yet my bones are aged and porous.

Caught up in the cocoon,
trapped in a self-enforced cell.
Pressure, anticipation, omnipresent,
all encompassing, waiting to emerge.
New and fresh and clean and healed.
A marvel for all to see.
Yet if forced or rushed then damage is ensured,
in equal measure to the illness of the past.

A pupa, a shell, held hostage.
And existing as a shadow.
Not the form or the essence of the past.
Not moving forward to a future.
Just trapped.
Surrounded by, and in a world that can't be
intercepted.

Who am I? What am I? Can I ever be anything
more than the affliction that I had?

Will it always define me?
Or can I live as an individual and not as a mind
diseased?

Permission to Breathe

I hereby bestow upon myself, permission to
breathe in air.
To allow myself forgiveness, to engage in
regular self-care.
To leave behind the baggage, and refrain from
negative self-harm,
To take tomorrow, fresh and new, without
discomfort or alarm.

I hereby grant permission to give myself just one
good day,
To move forwards, onwards, upwards - and keep
the dark thoughts firmly at bay.
To look for light and hope and even calm amidst
the wreck,
To not replay the damage already done, to give
myself some rest.

I know and feel acutely, how I almost died last
week,
And this reality is just as damaging as the events
I cannot speak.
So now I'm caught up in a cycle of dread, regret,
sorrow and despair,
Wishing to make progress, but more so willing
to repair.

So at present I sit in a limbo, trying so hard to
move on,
Yet my mind is determined to play tricks,
to deceive, to torture and to con.
I endeavour to give credit for the smallest of
good acts,
But at the close of play- can't always discern the
fiction from the fact.

Thus, I often fear I'm fighting a losing battle -
digging a hole deeper still,
Although fighting to hold on, feeling forever
weak and yet more ill.
I try to give myself the license to no longer be so
very lost,
But ultimately question -
if the trade off bears too high a cost?

Ode to A Tomato Plant

From a little seed,
I have watched you grow,
Bursting through the soil,
Ready! Emerging! Albeit slow.

I want to fast forward,
To the end and reward.
But know I must give you space,
To mature of your own accord.

It's easy to want andyearn to,
Skip to the end result.
Instant gratification,
Human nature - no fault.

But I see now on reflection,
It's patience I need.
Daily care and attention,
In fostering you to succeed.

You're just a tomato plant,
But symbolise so much more.
To nuture and nourish you,
Has made me explore.

The need and importance,
To just be as kind to myself.
Have self-compassion,
And leave self-sabotage on the shelf.

If I look at these past months,
We have truly grown together.
Sometimes faltering - in drought or excess,
But this won't be forever.

So as we both get stronger,
And continue to bloom,
I'll look after you,
And try to care for me too.

OCD: The Vexed Internal Monologue

I went through the scrubbing, washing of hands
on repeat,
Despite routine precisions, the need was never
complete.
And so painful, cracked and bleeding I covered
in bleach,
My red-raw fragile skin in an attempt to feel
clean.

But people would notice the behaviours and
signs,
Taps tightened, bathrooms locked in no time,
So the habits had to be hidden inside and not
out,
A visual action, but in mind carried out.

So the rituals became yet more covert by trade,
In turn the thoughts overtly screamed a tirade,
I could control the thought by scenarios played
out in my head,
But this transition gave no peace, just more
torment instead.

It's an impossible task to put the feeling away,
To get all boxes checked at the end of the day.

To have each thought finished, completed and
right,
Done and sorted, perfect and organised, out of
mind, out of sight.

The problem is that nothing ever feels done,
With each run of 3's, sets of 5, 9, 10 or 21s,
The repetitions almost make me feel worse,
Mounting anxiety, a cycle of patterns perverse.

It's an infinity, continuum, with no finite or end,
And yet my mind chases that coveted silence
pretend,
A mind field of fear – irrational wins over
logical thought,
Finding no pause, no break, no halting or stop.

It's a doubt, that's been magnified, squared
1000-fold times,
A parasite feeding on safety, peace, comfort and
kind,
The ill trust of self, the omnipotent dread,
Without checking or tapping my family could all
be dead.

It's the 'what ifs', the 'buts', the 'if onlys',
'shoulds' and 'coulds',
That torment my brain cells and dictate what I
do.

It's a stringently controlled paralysis of action,
No will, person, or feeling a greater force of
attraction.

It's debilitating, upsetting, overwhelming,
unjust,
To live with an illness that yourself cannot trust,
It takes over, and over, and over
And over, and over, and over,
And over, and over, and over again.
A vexed internal monologue,
on a loop,
With no end.

Goodbye OCD

I don't need you anymore.
Fact.
I can make a cup of tea and stir an even number,
or odd,and no-one will die today.
I can wash my hands for only the NHS
recommended length of time,
and know my family will be okay.

I no longer need to tap or switch the light
repeatedly off and on,
I can walk on cracks that won't 'break my back',
with the ease of chess board and moving pawn.
I no longer think the toothpaste is contaminated,
nor that there's poison in my tea.
The shower holds no chemicals - this I know -
and I can 'spend a penny' publicly.

I can eat a meal without the horrid rituals to
endure,
I may still face in battle daily,
but I want to be clear, resolute and sure.
In knowing I will never let you take so much life
again from me,
I have healed, am healing, and I will continue
until I'm free.

We had a close but dark relationship,
That I will admit.
Now I'm grateful I've moved on and am so
unburdened by the split.
So thank you for what you've taught me,
both of my brain and of my thoughts,
But respectfully I say goodbye,
you are not welcome,
pray forgot.

Iron Lung

Just breathe.
The pressure of an iron lung
Sits as a pain upon my heart
I cannot breathe alone
I cannot take in air
I cannot even start

The process to inhale
It bears just far too great a weight
With each intake and outbreath,
I question - is it a mistake?

Strike a match
To light a fire
And reignite my soul.
Because person, purpose, placement
Is lost - forgotten, desolate and cold.

Looking for an ember,
and finding only charred remains,
Seeking out the light,
Yet bound by, as yet, unyielding chains.

Ashes to ashes,
Dust to dust.
So burn my cast iron heart,
And leave it to rust.

Heart Beat

My heartbeat today.
My heartbeat,
for
the
very
first
time
today.

It has pumped with a pulse,
all other days until now.
It has had to.
But today –
there was the very first beat.

It was a staccato of still.
A cacophony of calm.
A resounding melody,
with a remedy,
to cure all former aches.

There was a present pentameter,
a rhythm,
a motion,
and an instrumental.
More than just a melancholic murmur.

A powerful palpitation,
and a propagation of purpose –
greater than the mere necessity,
to circulate blood and sustain life.

Today
I felt
my heart
beat –
for the very first time.

Wish to Remember. Will to Forget.

They're foggy and distant
And yet so focused and real
The torturous memories
On the journey to heal.

Often I wish to remember
And other times to forget
The feeling of torment that,
With each daybreak, I met.

And even in silence,
The dark quiet and sleep,
I face unwanted flashes
Of times I cannot yet speak.

Though the greatest of pains is
The question - was it all real?
The numbing of trauma
Frozen what I can feel.

So I wish to remember
And yet I will to forget
Which path leads to freedom?
That is not clear as of yet.

Farewell Little One

Farewell little one.
It's ok to let go.
You will be part of me always –
this you should know.
I have been moulded and formed,
with precious components of you.
Though I must [now] break free as a whole,
not be 'us' split in two.

Your pain was real,
and can still be haunting for me.
But we need not replay it,
in our minds, on nonstop repeat.

Yes, formative years lost,
and circumstances unjust.
But the heartache does not deserve.
to take yet more time away from us.

Little one, you've served your sentence,
and more than paid due debt.
Dry your tears one last instance,
the years have seen too many wept.

I am not you anymore,
though I hold you in my heart.

But for me to reach the finish line,
I must let go of the start.

We were never meant to hold onto the hurt so
tightly.
It should not torture waking hours, nor conjure
fear nightly.
Anguish cannot last a lifetime – not yours or
mine.
It's never meant to be forever – so though hard –
I'm going to try.

Little one, you are not the brittle one I used to
know.
You've survived and sometimes thrived – not
pressing stop but pushing go.
You've become me and I am growing, getting
stronger with each day.
But with my healing, means you disappearing,
and so it's important that I say.

I know it often doesn't seem like it
on the mornings when it feels you're making
sandwiches from crumbs.
Or the night-times that your breathing feels more
for fit for gills than lungs.
When head's above water, but still can barely
breathe,

although hard – those are the times, I need you
to most of all believe.

I will make it – on a foundation of trust and
faith,
Letting others in and not reliving the worst your
young days.
Let me give us permission to take a little weight
off of our chest,
Set down that load we've been carrying, and
give you – give us – some rest.
It need not last a minute more at this intensity,
I can work to live and breathe, and eventually
just be.

We [you and I],
can now have the fondest of goodbyes.
And in my parting words, say thank you,
for enduring, and ensuring I survived.

But little one, I feel it's now time to bid farewell.
My solo venture won't be easy,
but with conviction I can tell.
Tell you little one – I love you,
wish to protect you,
more than you'll ever know.
But the greatest gift I can give you [give us],
is of freedom.
And so I lovingly let you go.

I Tried

Why does my heart hurt?
Why can I not sleep?
Let me count the ways.

The duvet is too hot, heavy.
Sweat. Pouring out liquid emotions I can't
express in daylight.
But I'm cold. In body and heart. Distant – frozen
in time.
Too warm, too cold, too much grey malady of in
between.
Too much of everything and never enough of
anything.
Restless and relentless.

Why?
Many things.
Because I said a line wrong in a primary school
play.
I forgot my parents' wedding anniversary.
I wet the bed aged 12 and 15 and even at 17.
Fear and terror.

I lost a post-it with my shopping list.
I said 'you too' when the context made no sense.
I dropped my drink when I was sober.
I dropped my drinks when I was drunk.

I misjudged a hug as a kiss on the cheek.

I got my change wrong.
I left my hair a day too long before washing.
I lied about a band I knew – but had never heard
of.
I missed a deadline.
I missed another.

I drank milk 4 days out of date.
I cried because my heart was beating too fast.
I cried because it was beating too slowly.
I forgot to post a birthday card

I wore the same underwear 2 [3] days in a row...
I spilled my coffee.
All over my computer.
And my emotions came pouring out on the keys.

I ordered take-away because I had no clean
dishes.
I ordered takeaway because the effort to cook
was overwhelming
I ordered takeaway and it sat for days in the
fridge.
Because the effort to eat was too much.
I ordered takeaway – for the sake of ordering
takeaway.
Because it gave me some sense of human
purpose...

At the very least – need.

I smiled when I answered the door.
I smiled when I needed to burst.
I smiled when all my body could do was cry.

I said I was okay when it couldn't be further
from the truth.
I missed the bus.
I missed everything.

I didn't meet the objective.
I turned up late [again].
I slept in.
I sent emails at 5am.

I said the wrong things.
I didn't take the bin out.
I fell asleep fully clothed.
I used a disposable straw – despite ethics – and
what I believe and know.

I tried to look for answers – in a treasure chest
absent of coins.
I tried to be a person.
I tried to be an example.
I tried to be.

I tried.

There is a Light, There is a Door

Have you ever felt so empty?
That you've forgotten how to breathe?
So weak without resolve,
That you just buckle to your knees?

That even when you're outside,
There just isn't enough air.
Of all emotions rushing by,
All your hand grasps is despair.

Have you ever felt so desperate?
Like your whole world's caving in?
So no matter how you push and strive,
It appears you'll never win.

When the odds seem stacked against you,
And there's nowhere left to go.
When you're surrounded by people,
And yet feel increasingly alone.

Have you ever felt so hopeless?
And that life has no value left?
Whereby, fighting to hold on,
Just leaves you bankrupt and bereft?

Well I'm here to try and tell you,
That I know this feeling well.
And – I acknowledge this admission,
Won't serve to calm or ease your hell.

But what I wish you to believe is,
That it won't last forevermore.
Although now, feeling never-ending,
There's a light and there's a door.

Yes, the door is hard to open,
And you can't do it by yourself.
It's heavy, rusted, barred and bolted,
So you're going to need some help.

Now help is an endless resource,
If…you know how and where to look.
I know you're broken and exhausted,
So this will take one lasting push.

But, in reaching out you'll have made,
The first step – from darkness into light.
Yes, it may appear so grey now,
The change won't happen overnight.

But with help, support and love,
I promise the smog will begin to clear.
And with time, and more time yet again,
The light will start to near.

The door will open slowly,
Don't force it – or you might get hurt.
Gentle, little movements,
Conserve strength, rather than exert.

The helping hands will push,
With you, to ease and support the strain.
Now – the door may swing back sometimes –
Don't give up, start over again.

With help and time and input,
The door will allow you to pass through.
Where things seem a little brighter,
The air less dense – more fresh and new.

You'll look back and remember,
When you thought, you'd never make it there.
And know now – how very far you've come,
That broken parts can be repaired.

So – if you are, or ever find yourself,
Lost and feeling in this way.
Remember there's a light, there's a door,
And they will not be too far away.

Full Circle

I'm used to spirals into pits of despair,
Even triangles, hierarchies, of needs and care.
I know boxes, that I've been confined to, or
placed myself in,
Ticks, more often crosses – with those I'm akin.
But this unfamiliar shape – is a circle – one of
hope,
Not leading to torment or anguish bespoke.
This is a circle, of positive, progress and change,
I've come full circle,
and it wasn't in vain.